CCSS **Genre** Expository T

MW00965296

Essential Question
How do animals adapt to challenges in
their habitat?

Life in a Tide Pool

by Mary Mackie

Chapter 1

A Changing World

If you take a walk along a rocky shoreline and look closely at the indentations in the rocks, you will see a whole world of creatures. Clusters of mussels, limpets, and small snails cling to rocks. The **tentacles** of the green sea anemone wave underwater. Sea stars and spiky sea urchins show their colors. Crabs conceal themselves beneath rocks.

The animals in a tide pool live in a constantly changing environment. Twice a day, ocean water rushes in and covers the land. Then the water rushes out again, exposing the rocks and sand. Small pools of water are left behind, but the rest of the shore remains dry.

Tide pool creatures live in a constantly changing environment.

The small pools of water along the shoreline are called tide pools. Tide pools form in rocky areas where the land meets the sea. For example, one place that is known for its tide pools is along the rocky coast of California.

A tide pool is a **habitat** for many different plants and animals. A habitat is the type of environment in which plants or animals naturally live. Forests, deserts, and oceans are all types of habitat. Because tide pools are found along the coasts of oceans they are a type of coastal habitat.

Crabs live in tide pools on rocky coasts.

The level of the ocean's water where it meets the land is constantly changing. The ocean rises and falls regularly along the coast. The term "tide" refers to this regular rise and fall. The tide pool habitat forms between the lowest low tides and the highest high tides. This area is called the intertidal zone.

The intertidal zone can be divided into four smaller zones: the low tide zone, the mid zone, the high tide zone, and the splash zone. The low tide zone is mostly underwater. It is only exposed when the tide is very low. The mid zone is exposed twice a day by the tides. The high tide zone is flooded at high tide. The splash zone is dry most of the time, but is splashed with salt water during high tides.

Tide pools change as the tide rises and falls.

High Tide and Low Tide

The tides are the periodic rise and fall of the ocean or other large bodies of water. The tide rises and falls twice a day. High tide occurs when the rising tide reaches its maximum height. Low tide occurs when the falling tide reaches its lowest level.

Intertidal Zone Map

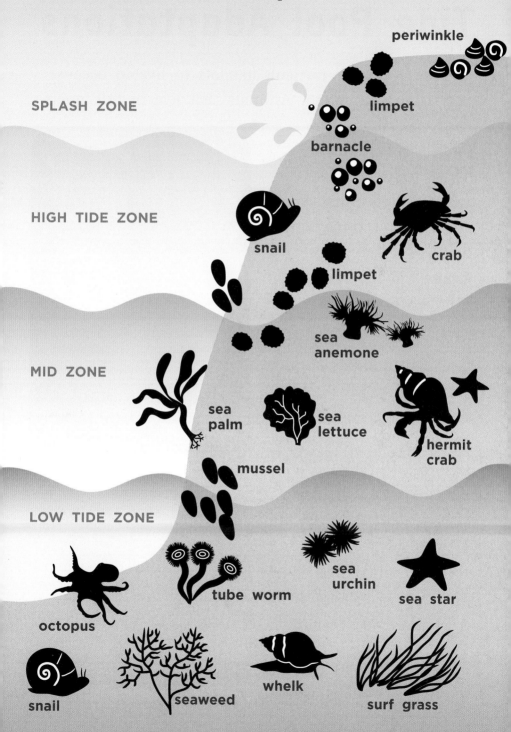

SPLASH ZONE

HIGH TIDE ZONE

MID ZONE

LOW TIDE ZONE

periwinkle

limpet

barnacle

snail

crab

limpet

sea anemone

sea palm

sea lettuce

hermit crab

mussel

octopus

tube worm

sea urchin

sea star

snail

seaweed

whelk

surf grass

5

Chapter 2

Tide Pool Adaptations

Tide pools are difficult habitats to live in because they change so often. Animals that live in tide pools need special features to help them survive. These features are called **adaptations**. An adaptation is often a body part that helps an animal obtain food, build a home, or keep safe.

Some adaptations help tide pool animals survive both in the water and out of the water. A sea anemone has more than one adaptation to help it survive. When it is covered by water, the sea anemone looks like a

Sea anemones have a sucker disk that helps them stay in place even when they are hit by strong waves.

flower. It waves its long tentacles in the water trying to catch fish. But when the tide pool is dry, the anemone changes. It hides its tentacles from the sun by pulling them into its body. The anemone also has a sucker disk that keeps it fastened to a rock so that strong waves can't wash it out to sea.

Barnacles, limpets, and mussels have adaptations to help them survive in the splash zone. Because they are in the sun for much of the day, they have hard shells for protection from the sun's rays. They are able to store water and food inside their shells. The shells also protect them from **predators**. Other animals that have shells for shelter and protection include snails, crabs, and hermit crabs.

Barnacles, limpets, and mussels have adapted to life in the splash zone. They have hard shells that protect them from the sun.

Sea hares are well camouflaged,
making them hard to see among
the rocks in a tide pool.

Sometimes one adaptation is not enough. California sea hares, or sea slugs, live in the mid and low tide zones. They feed on algae and seaweed. To protect themselves from sun and waves they can shrink their soft bodies and hide between rocks.

The sea hare also has ways to protect itself from predators. Its brown, spotted color allows it to fool predators by looking like a tide pool rock. If a predator does come too close, the sea hare shoots out purple ink. The ink forms a cloud that blinds the predator, allowing the sea hare to get away.

Sea urchins are related to sea stars. Like sea stars, sea urchins have hundreds of sticky tube feet. The tube feet help them to grab food. Unlike sea stars, sea urchins eat only plants. They have hard teeth to scrape plants from rocks. They also use their hard teeth to grind rocks. They make a hollow in the rocks to use as a home.

Sea urchins are covered in long, movable spines that help these slow-moving animals to walk. The spines are sharp and contain poison. The spines and the poison keep predators away.

The sea star (left) and the sea urchin come from the same family. They have some of the same features, such as their sticky tube feet.

Physical features such as special body parts are not the only types of adaptation that tide pool animals have. Behavior can also be an adaptation. Many tide pool animals try to fool predators with their behavior. For example, some crabs bury themselves in sand. A crab called the decorator crab even decorates its shell with seaweed and small shells to keep from being seen!

Sea stars and other tide pool predators often feed on mussels. To protect themselves, mussels gather in large groups to stay safe. Periwinkles, oysters, and sand-castle worms also gather together in large groups for protection.

Decorator crabs camouflage themselves so that they can disappear among the shells and seaweed in a tide pool.

A sand-castle worm uses its tentacles to catch food such as plankton.

Mussels live next to each other in beds, with each mussel attaching itself to the rock separately. They do not join their shells together. In contrast, sand-castle worms live together by building one large group home called a colony. A sand-castle worm colony resembles a honeycomb. It is made up of many tubes joined together. Each tube houses a sand-castle worm. The worms stay in their tubes and are almost never seen. When the tide comes in and covers the colony, the worms use their tentacles to catch food that is floating in the water.

A Special Glue

Sand-castle worms have a special adaptation that helps them build their tubes. First, the worm collects something like a piece of shell. Then, an organ on its head pushes a blob of glue out onto the shell. The worm wiggles the shell into place and lets the glue set.

Chapter 3

Tide Pool Predators

There are many predators living in tide pools, which leads to a lot of competition for food. Some tide pool animals have adaptations that make them more successful at catching and eating **prey**.

Sea stars live on rocks around the tide pool. They move slowly over the rocks on special tube feet that have sticky suction cups. Their feet help them to cling to rocks. They stop the sea stars from being washed away.

Sea stars feed on shellfish that live on the rocks, such as mussels, oysters, and clams. Sea stars usually swallow small prey whole. They have an amazing way of feeding on larger prey. They use their sticky feet to open the mussel shells. Then they push their stomach out through their mouth and into the mussel's shell and eat the prey.

Sea stars have hundreds of tube-like feet tipped with sticky suction cups.

The octopus is a very successful tide pool predator. An octopus cannot survive out of the water, so it stays close to the low tide zone or swims in the open ocean. It prefers life in the low tide zone, where it can feed on crabs, snails, and clams.

An octopus has excellent adaptations to help it catch prey. It can change the color of its skin to make it look like the rocks or sand around it. It can squeeze its soft body into narrow cracks. Once hidden, the octopus waits, staying alert for small animals passing by. Then it uses its tentacles to grab its prey.

The octopus has eight tentacles, each with a row of strong suckers. The suckers help the octopus to grab its prey.

An octopus is a master of disguise. It can hide in a tide pool by changing color to look like the sand and rocks around it.

We need to be careful when visiting tide pools. People visit tide pools for many reasons. Some people want to study them and learn about the creatures that live there. Some people collect tide pool creatures like sea urchins and mussels for food. Some people and their pets walk through tide pools. All of these activities can harm the creatures that live there.

To help the creatures in the tide pool environment survive, we should always remember to leave the tide pool exactly as we found it.

The creatures that live in tide pools often have to share their space with humans. We should always be careful not to damage their environment.

Summarize

Use details from *Life in a Tide Pool* to summarize the selection. The graphic organizer may help you.

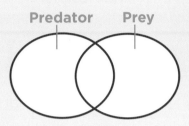

Text Evidence

1. How do you know that *Life in a Tide Pool* is an expository text? GENRE

2. What features do sea stars and sea urchins have in common? What features do they have that are different? COMPARE AND CONTRAST

3. What does the word *survive* on page 6 mean? Rewrite the sentence to mean the same thing, but use a different word or phrase to replace the word *survive*. SENTENCE CLUES

4. Compare an octopus with another tide pool animal. Describe the features they share and those that are different. WRITE ABOUT READING

Compare Texts

Read how the bluebird and the coyote got their colors.

Bluebird and Coyote

Did you know that bluebirds were not always blue? In fact, the first bluebird was brown. Then, one night, the bluebird had a dream.

"Bored with brown?" a voice asked. "It's not too late to change. Just visit the blue lake."

"Is it far?" asked the bluebird, for he was lazy.

"Yes, very far," said the voice. "But it's worth the trip. Just bathe in the lake for five mornings and your feathers will turn a brilliant blue. You will also be very clean."

"Is that all? It seems too easy," said the bluebird suspiciously.

"Oh, right, I almost forgot," said the voice. "Sing the 'Ode to Blue' while you are bathing in the lake."

"What are the words to 'Ode to Blue'?" asked Bluebird.

"Just make them up as you go," said the voice.

Bluebird did as he was told, and all was well until the fourth morning, when all of his feathers fell out.

"Can this be right?" he asked, but there was nobody there to hear him. Or so he thought.

To Bluebird's great relief, on the fifth morning, when he emerged from the lake, he had beautiful blue feathers.

Meanwhile, a coyote was watching. He had hoped to snack on Bluebird, but  seeing those bright blue feathers gave him other ideas.

"How did you do that?" asked Coyote. "You were so drab, but now you look amazing. I want that color!"

Did I mention that Coyote was green?

"Here's what you do," said Bluebird.

Coyote followed the instructions faithfully. His "Ode to Blue" was magnificent, and he sang for hours. On the fourth day, his fur fell out, which bothered him a little. He was thrilled when, on the fifth day, it grew back and it was electric blue.

"Excellent color!" said Coyote. He pranced along the road, checking all the time to see who was looking at him.

"How can they not admire me?" he asked himself. "I am the blue coyote, first of my kind!"

Eager to see if his shadow was as beautiful as he was, Coyote whipped his head around. But he never learned the answer to that question.

Bang! Coyote ran straight into a tree branch! Stunned, he fell to the ground and was soon covered in brown dust. Since that day, there has never been a blue coyote, but coyotes still howl a few verses of "Ode to Blue" at the end of the day. Just in case.

Make Connections

In *Bluebird and Coyote,* Coyote turns blue. Would that be a useful adaptation for a coyote?
ESSENTIAL QUESTION

How does being able to change color help some tide pool animals? How does being brown help a coyote? TEXT TO TEXT

Glossary

adaptations *(ad-ap-TAY-shuhnz)* changes in animals or plants that fit them better for their environment *(page 6)*

behavior *(bee-HAYV-yuhr)* the way in which something behaves *(page 10)*

habitat *(HAB-ih-tat)* the place where a plant or animal naturally lives or grows *(page 3)*

physical *(FIZ-i-kuhl)* to do with the body *(page 10)*

predators *(PRED-uh-turz)* animals that eat other animals *(page 7)*

prey *(PRAY)* animals that are eaten by other animals *(page 12)*

tentacles *(TEN-tuh-kuhlz)* long, flexible animal parts used for grasping or feeling *(page 2)*

Index

Focus on Science

Purpose To compare and contrast animals by their adaptations.

What to Do

Step 1 Make a list of eight animals that you read about in *Life in a Tide Pool.*

Step 2 Create a three-column chart with the following headings.

Animal	Where They Live	Type of Adaptation

Step 3 Place each animal from your list in the correct column on the chart. For example, note the specific part of the intertidal zone where each animal lives.

Step 4 Brainstorm more animals and add them to the chart. Research where they live and the type of adaptations they have.

Conclusion What can you learn by comparing and contrasting animals this way?